CONTENTS

Medical Disclaimer

The information provided in this e-book is for general informational purposes only and is not intended as a substitute for professional medical advice, diagnosis, or treatment. Always seek the advice of your physician or other qualified health provider with any questions you may have regarding a medical condition or mental health issue.

Never disregard professional medical advice or delay in seeking it because of something you have read in this e-book. The author and publisher of this e-book are not responsible for any adverse effects or consequences resulting from the use of any suggestions, products, or procedures described herein.

If you are experiencing a medical or mental health emergency, please call your doctor or emergency services immediately. The use of any information provided in this e-book is solely at your own risk.

Copyright Notice

"THE ART OF MENTAL SELF-CARE: CULTIVATING A THRIVING MINDSET"

Introduction

- Importance of mental well-being
- Overview of the eBook

Chapter 1: Understanding Mental Well-Being

- Definition and importance
- Common misconceptions
- Factors affecting mental well-being

Chapter 2: Recognizing the Signs

- Symptoms of poor mental well-being
- How to identify when you need support
- Case studies and real-life examples

Chapter 3: Building a Strong Foundation

- The role of physical health
- Nutrition and mental well-being
- Importance of sleep

Chapter 4: Mindfulness and Meditation
- Introduction to mindfulness
- Benefits of meditation
- Practical exercises and techniques

Chapter 5: Emotional Intelligence
- Understanding and managing emotions
- Building resilience
- Developing empathy and improving relationships

Chapter 6: Stress Management
- Identifying sources of stress
- Effective stress reduction techniques
- Creating a balanced lifestyle

Chapter 7: Social Connections and Support

- The importance of community
- Building and maintaining healthy relationships

- Seeking professional help when needed

Chapter 8: Personal Growth and Fulfillment

- Setting goals and finding purpose
- Developing a positive mindset
- Continuous learning and self-improvement

Chapter 9: Technology and Mental Well-Being

- The impact of social media
- Setting healthy boundaries with technology
- Utilizing apps and tools for well-being

Chapter 10: Creating a Personalized Mental Well-Being Plan

- Assessing your current state
- Setting realistic and achievable goals
- Monitoring progress and making adjustments

The Impact of Lifestyle Choices on Mental Well-Being

Conclusion

- Recap of key points
- Encouragement for ongoing self-care
- Resources for further reading and support

Dear Reader,

Thank you for taking the time to explore this e-book on mental well-being. I am truly grateful for your commitment to understanding and enhancing your mental health and overall well-being. It is my hope that the insights and strategies shared within these pages serve as a valuable resource on your journey to a more balanced and fulfilling life.

Your dedication to self-care and personal growth is commendable, and I encourage you to continue applying these principles and exploring new ways to nurture your mental well-being. Remember, this journey is ongoing, and every step you take towards self-improvement is a step towards a healthier, happier you.

If you have found this book helpful, please consider sharing it with others who might benefit from it. Your support and feedback are deeply appreciated and contribute to the ongoing effort to promote mental well-being and self-care.

You can also follow as on social media platform;Social media links :

Instagram:https://www.instagram.com/justbeyou_online? igsh=czRvMzZrN29zdW5h

Facebook:https://www.facebook.com/profile.php? id=100091418682151&mibextid=ZbWKwL

Tweeter:https://x.com/msodi31?s=09

Website:https://justbeyou-online.com

Thank you once again for your time and engagement. Wishing you continued growth, resilience, and a life filled with well-being and joy.

Warm regards, [M.kaur]

"THE ART OF MENTAL SELF-CARE: CULTIVATING A THRIVING MINDSET"

Introduction

Welcome to "Nurturing Your Mind: A Guide to Mental Well-Being." In a world that constantly demands our attention and energy, it's easy to overlook the importance of our mental well-being. Just as we care for our physical health, nurturing our mind is crucial for leading a balanced and fulfilling life. This eBook aims to provide you with practical insights, tools, and strategies to enhance your mental well-being, helping you to thrive in every aspect of your life.

Mental well-being is not just the absence of mental illness but a state of overall happiness and contentment. It encompasses our emotions, thoughts, and behaviors, influencing how we handle stress, relate to others, and make choices. By understanding and prioritizing our mental well-being, we can improve our resilience, build stronger relationships, and achieve a greater sense of purpose.

Throughout this eBook, we will explore various aspects of mental well-being, from recognizing the signs of distress to building a strong foundation for a healthy mind. Each chapter is designed to offer practical advice and actionable steps, empowering you to take charge of your mental well-being and lead a more balanced life.

Let's embark on this journey together, learning how to nurture our minds and unlock our full potential.

CHAPTER 1: UNDERSTANDING MENTAL WELL-BEING

Definition and Importance

Mental well-being is a state of mental health that enables individuals to cope with the normal stresses of life, work productively, and contribute to their communities. It is characterized by emotional stability, positive relationships, and a sense of purpose. Mental well-being is essential for overall health, as it influences how we think, feel, and act.

Good mental well-being helps us to:

- Build and maintain healthy relationships
- Cope with stress and adversity
- Achieve personal and professional goals
- Enjoy life and appreciate the world around us

Common Misconceptions

There are several misconceptions about mental well-being that can prevent people from seeking help or making positive changes. Let's address some of these myths:

- **Myth 1: Mental well-being is only about being happy all the time.**
Reality: Mental well-being includes experiencing a range of emotions, both positive and negative. It's about managing these emotions effectively and maintaining a balance.
- **Myth 2: Mental well-being is only important for those with mental illness.**
Reality: Everyone benefits from good mental well-being. It is crucial for overall health and quality of life.
- **Myth 3: Improving mental well-being requires drastic changes.**
Reality: Small, consistent steps can make a significant difference in enhancing mental well-being.

Factors Affecting Mental Well-Being

Several factors can influence our mental well-being.

Understanding these can help us take proactive steps to improve our mental health.

- **Biological Factors:** Genetics, brain chemistry, and physical health play a role in mental well-being. While we can't change our genetic makeup, we can take steps to improve our physical health through diet, exercise, and sleep.
- **Psychological Factors:** Our thoughts, emotions, and coping mechanisms significantly impact our mental well-being. Developing positive thinking patterns and healthy coping strategies can enhance our mental health.
- **Social Factors:** Relationships and social support systems are crucial for mental well-being. Building and maintaining positive relationships with family, friends, and communities can provide a sense of belonging and support.
- **Environmental Factors:** Our surroundings, including our home, work, and community environments, can influence our mental well-being. Creating a positive and supportive environment can help reduce stress and promote mental health.

In the following chapters, we will delve deeper into these factors and explore practical ways to improve our mental well-being. By understanding and addressing these elements, we can create a solid foundation for a healthier, happier mind.

CHAPTER 2: RECOGNIZING THE SIGNS

Symptoms of Poor Mental Well-Being

Recognizing the signs of poor mental well-being is the first step towards improving it. Symptoms can vary widely, but some common indicators include:

- **Emotional Symptoms:**
  - Persistent sadness or depression
  - Feelings of hopelessness or helplessness
  - Increased irritability or mood swings
  - Anxiety or excessive worry
- **Behavioral Symptoms:**
  - Withdrawal from social activities
  - Changes in sleeping patterns (insomnia or oversleeping)
  - Changes in eating habits (loss of appetite or overeating)
  - Substance abuse (alcohol, drugs, etc.)
- **Physical Symptoms:**
  - Unexplained aches and pains
  - Chronic fatigue or lack of energy
  - Frequent illnesses or weakened immune system
- **Cognitive Symptoms:**
  - Difficulty concentrating or making decisions

- o Memory problems
- o Negative thought patterns

Recognizing these symptoms early can help in seeking timely support and taking steps to improve mental well-being.

How to Identify When You Need Support

It's important to know when to seek help for mental well-being. Here are some signs that indicate you might need professional support:

- **Persistent Symptoms:** If emotional, behavioral, physical, or cognitive symptoms persist for more than two weeks, it might be time to seek help.
- **Impact on Daily Life:** If symptoms are interfering with your ability to work, study, or maintain relationships, professional support can be beneficial.
- **Difficulty Coping:** If you find it hard to cope with stress or daily challenges, reaching out for help can provide you with the necessary tools and strategies.
- **Thoughts of Self-Harm:** If you are experiencing thoughts of self-harm or suicide, it's crucial to seek immediate help from a mental health professional or crisis hotline.

Case Studies and Real-Life Examples

Understanding real-life experiences can make the journey towards better mental well-being more relatable. Here are a few case studies:

- **Case Study 1: Sarah's Journey with Anxiety**
  Sarah, a 28-year-old graphic designer, started experiencing severe anxiety after moving to a new city for work. She noticed persistent worry, difficulty sleeping, and social withdrawal. Recognizing these signs, Sarah sought help from a therapist who taught her cognitive-behavioral techniques to manage her anxiety. With time, Sarah learned to cope with her anxiety and improved her overall mental well-being.

- **Case Study 2: John's Battle with Depression**

John, a 45-year-old teacher, began feeling overwhelmingly sad and hopeless after a personal loss. He lost interest in activities he once enjoyed and struggled to get out of bed. Realizing the impact on his daily life, John reached out to a mental health professional. Through a combination of therapy and medication, John gradually regained his sense of purpose and improved his mental health.

- **Case Study 3: Maria's Experience with Burnout**

Maria, a 35-year-old nurse, felt constantly exhausted and disconnected from her work due to the demands of her job. She recognized signs of burnout and decided to make changes. Maria started practicing self-care, setting boundaries, and seeking support from colleagues and friends. These steps helped her regain energy and passion for her work.

These examples highlight the importance of recognizing the signs of poor mental well-being and taking proactive steps to address them. Seeking support, whether from friends, family, or professionals, can make a significant difference in improving mental health.

In the next chapter, we will explore how to build a strong foundation for mental well-being by focusing on physical health, nutrition, and sleep.

CHAPTER 3:
BUILDING A STRONG FOUNDATION

The Role of Physical Health

Physical health and mental well-being are closely linked. A healthy body can enhance mood, increase energy levels, and improve overall mental health. Here are some key aspects of physical health that impact mental well-being:

- **Exercise:** Regular physical activity releases endorphins, which are natural mood lifters. Exercise also reduces stress, improves sleep, and boosts self-esteem. Aim for at least 30 minutes of moderate exercise most days of the week. Activities like walking, jogging, swimming, yoga, or dancing can be beneficial.
- **Nutrition:** A balanced diet provides the nutrients necessary for brain function and emotional regulation. Here are some dietary tips for better mental well-being:
  - **Eat a Variety of Foods:** Include fruits, vegetables, whole grains, lean proteins, and healthy fats in your diet.
  - **Stay Hydrated:** Drink plenty of water throughout the day.
  - **Limit Processed Foods and Sugars:** These can lead to mood swings and energy crashes.
  - **Include Omega-3 Fatty Acids:** Found in fish, flaxseeds,

and walnuts, omega-3s support brain health.

- **Sleep:** Quality sleep is crucial for mental well-being. Poor sleep can exacerbate symptoms of anxiety and depression. Here are some tips for better sleep:
  - **Establish a Routine:** Go to bed and wake up at the same time every day.
  - **Create a Relaxing Environment:** Keep your bedroom cool, dark, and quiet.
  - **Limit Screen Time Before Bed:** The blue light from screens can interfere with sleep. Try to avoid screens for at least an hour before bedtime.
  - **Practice Relaxation Techniques:** Activities like reading, meditating, or taking a warm bath can help you unwind before bed.

Importance of Sleep

Sleep is essential for mental and physical health. During sleep, the body repairs itself, and the brain processes emotions and memories. Lack of sleep can impair cognitive function, increase stress, and negatively impact mood. Here's how to ensure you get enough rest:

- **Understand Your Sleep Needs:** Most adults need 7-9 hours of sleep per night. Listen to your body and adjust your sleep schedule accordingly.
- **Develop a Sleep Routine:** Consistency helps regulate your body's internal clock. Establish a bedtime routine that includes calming activities.
- **Create a Sleep-Friendly Environment:** Make your bedroom conducive to sleep by keeping it cool, dark, and free from distractions.
- **Manage Stress:** High stress levels can interfere with sleep. Practice stress-reduction techniques such as deep breathing, meditation, or journaling.

Creating Healthy Habits

Building a strong foundation for mental well-being

involves creating and maintaining healthy habits. Here are some tips to help you get started:

- **Set Realistic Goals:** Start with small, achievable goals that can be gradually increased over time. For example, aim to walk for 10 minutes a day and gradually increase the duration.
- **Track Your Progress:** Keeping a journal or using an app to track your habits can help you stay motivated and see your progress.
- **Find Activities You Enjoy:** Choose physical activities and foods that you enjoy to make it easier to stick with your new habits.
- **Stay Flexible:** Life can be unpredictable, and it's okay to adjust your routine as needed. The key is to remain consistent and not give up.
- **Seek Support:** Share your goals with friends or family members who can offer encouragement and accountability.

By focusing on physical health, nutrition, and sleep, you can build a strong foundation for mental well-being. These habits not only improve your mood and energy levels but also enhance your ability to cope with stress and challenges.

In the next chapter, we will explore mindfulness and meditation, powerful tools for enhancing mental well-being.

CHAPTER 4: MINDFULNESS AND MEDITATION

Introduction to Mindfulness

Mindfulness is the practice of being fully present in the moment, aware of where we are and what we're doing, and not overly reactive or overwhelmed by what's happening around us. It involves paying attention to our thoughts, feelings, bodily sensations, and surrounding environment with an open, non-judgmental attitude.

The benefits of mindfulness include:

- Reduced stress and anxiety
- Improved focus and concentration
- Enhanced emotional regulation
- Greater self-awareness
- Improved relationships

Benefits of Meditation

Meditation is a practice where an individual uses a technique—such as mindfulness, or focusing the mind on a particular object, thought, or activity—to train attention and awareness and achieve a mentally clear and emotionally calm state. Here are some benefits of regular meditation:

- **Stress Reduction:** Meditation lowers the levels of the

stress hormone cortisol, reducing stress and anxiety.

- **Improved Concentration:** Regular meditation practice can improve attention span and focus.
- **Emotional Health:** Meditation can lead to an improved self-image and a more positive outlook on life.
- **Self-Awareness:** Meditation increases awareness of self and surroundings, fostering better understanding and acceptance of oneself.
- **Lengthened Attention Span:** Focused-attention meditation helps increase the strength and endurance of your attention.

Practical Exercises and Techniques

Here are some mindfulness and meditation techniques to help you get started:

1. **Mindful Breathing:** Sit comfortably and focus your attention on your breath. Notice the sensation of the air entering and leaving your nostrils. When your mind wanders, gently bring your focus back to your breath.
2. **Body Scan Meditation:** Lie down comfortably and slowly focus your attention on different parts of your body, starting from your toes and moving up to your head. Notice any sensations, tension, or discomfort without trying to change anything.
3. **Loving-Kindness Meditation:** Sit comfortably and focus on your breath. Once relaxed, silently repeat phrases like "May I be happy, may I be healthy, may I be safe, may I live with ease." Gradually extend these wishes to others in your life.
4. **Mindful Walking:** Walk slowly and pay attention to the physical sensation of walking. Notice how your feet feel as they touch the ground, how your legs move, and the rhythm of your steps.
5. **Guided Meditation:** Use apps or online resources that offer guided meditations. These can provide structure and support, especially if you are new to meditation.

6.   **Five Senses Exercise:** Take a moment to pause and focus on the present moment by noticing:
   - Five things you can see
   - Four things you can feel
   - Three things you can hear
   - Two things you can smell
   - One thing you can taste

Incorporating Mindfulness into Daily Life

Mindfulness can be integrated into daily routines to enhance overall well-being. Here are some simple ways to practice mindfulness throughout the day:

- **Mindful Eating:** Pay full attention to the experience of eating. Notice the colors, smells, textures, and flavors of your food. Eat slowly and savor each bite.
- **Mindful Listening:** When talking to someone, give them your full attention. Listen without planning your response and notice their words, tone, and body language.
- **Mindful Breaks:** Take short breaks during the day to practice mindful breathing or stretching. This can help reduce stress and improve focus.
- **Mindful Chores:** Turn everyday tasks like washing dishes or cleaning into mindfulness practices. Focus on the sensations, movements, and sounds involved in the activity.
- **Mindful Transitions:** Use transitions between activities, such as walking to your car or waiting for an appointment, as opportunities to practice mindfulness.

By incorporating mindfulness and meditation into your routine, you can cultivate a greater sense of calm, clarity, and emotional balance. These practices can help you navigate life's challenges with more resilience and grace.

In the next chapter, we will explore emotional intelligence, focusing on understanding and managing emotions to enhance mental well-being.

CHAPTER 5: EMOTIONAL INTELLIGENCE

Understanding Emotional Intelligence

Emotional intelligence (EI) is the ability to understand, manage, and use your own emotions in positive ways to relieve stress, communicate effectively, empathize with others, overcome challenges, and defuse conflict. It involves four key components:

1. **Self-Awareness:** Recognizing your own emotions and how they affect your thoughts and behavior. Understanding your strengths and weaknesses, and having self-confidence.
2. **Self-Management:** Being able to control impulsive feelings and behaviors, manage your emotions in healthy ways, take initiative, follow through on commitments, and adapt to changing circumstances.
3. **Social Awareness:** Understanding the emotions, needs, and concerns of other people, picking up on emotional cues, feeling comfortable socially, and recognizing the dynamics in a group or organization.
4. **Relationship Management:** Knowing how to develop and maintain good relationships, communicate clearly, inspire and influence others,

work well in a team, and manage conflict.

Building Resilience

Resilience is the ability to recover from setbacks, adapt well to change, and keep going in the face of adversity. Here are some strategies to build resilience:

- **Maintain a Positive Outlook:** Focus on what you can control and let go of what you can't. Practice gratitude and look for opportunities for personal growth in difficult situations.
- **Develop Strong Relationships:** Building a network of supportive relationships can provide a buffer against stress. Share your feelings with trusted friends or family members and seek support when needed.
- **Take Care of Yourself:** Prioritize self-care activities that nurture your body and mind. Exercise, eat well, get enough sleep, and make time for activities you enjoy.
- **Learn from Experience:** Reflect on past experiences and identify what helped you get through difficult times. Use this knowledge to develop new coping strategies.
- **Stay Flexible:** Be open to change and willing to adapt your plans as needed. Flexibility can help you navigate challenges more effectively.

Developing Empathy and Improving Relationships

Empathy is the ability to understand and share the feelings of another person. It is a crucial component of emotional intelligence and can strengthen relationships. Here are some ways to develop empathy:

- **Listen Actively:** Pay full attention to the person speaking, without interrupting. Show that you are listening through nodding, making eye contact, and responding appropriately.
- **Put Yourself in Their Shoes:** Try to see the situation from the other person's perspective. Ask yourself how you would feel in their position and what might be motivating their behavior.

- **Ask Questions:** Show genuine interest in the other person's experiences and feelings. Ask open-ended questions to encourage them to share more.
- **Validate Their Feelings:** Acknowledge the other person's emotions, even if you don't agree with their perspective. Validation shows that you respect and understand their feelings.

Improving your relationships involves practicing empathy, effective communication, and conflict resolution. Here are some tips:

- **Communicate Clearly:** Express your thoughts and feelings openly and honestly, while being respectful and considerate of others.
- **Set Boundaries:** Establish and maintain healthy boundaries in your relationships to protect your well-being.
- **Resolve Conflicts Constructively:** Approach conflicts with a willingness to understand the other person's perspective and find a mutually acceptable solution.
- **Show Appreciation:** Regularly express gratitude and appreciation for the people in your life. Acknowledge their contributions and positive qualities.

Practical Exercises

Here are some exercises to help you develop emotional intelligence:

1. **Self-Reflection Journal:** Spend a few minutes each day reflecting on your emotions and reactions. Write about situations that triggered strong emotions and explore what caused those feelings. Consider how you responded and what you could do differently in the future.
2. **Mindful Emotion Check-In:** Set aside a few moments throughout the day to check in with your emotions. Pause and take a few deep breaths. Notice what

you are feeling and where you feel it in your body. Acknowledge your emotions without judgment.

3. **Empathy Practice:** Choose a person in your life and imagine a recent situation they experienced. Try to put yourself in their shoes and understand their emotions and perspective. Reflect on how you might respond with empathy and support.

4. **Active Listening Exercise:** Practice active listening with a friend or family member. Focus entirely on what they are saying without planning your response. After they finish speaking, summarize what you heard to ensure understanding and show that you were listening.

5. **Gratitude Journal:** Each day, write down three things you are grateful for and why. This practice can help shift your focus to positive aspects of your life and improve your overall outlook.

By developing emotional intelligence, you can enhance your ability to understand and manage your emotions, build stronger relationships, and improve your overall mental well-being.

In the next chapter, we will explore effective stress management techniques to help you create a balanced and fulfilling life.

CHAPTER 6: STRESS MANAGEMENT

Identifying Sources of Stress

Understanding what causes your stress is the first step in managing it effectively. Common sources of stress include:

- **Work:** High workloads, tight deadlines, job insecurity, or conflicts with colleagues.
- **Relationships:** Arguments with loved ones, family responsibilities, or lack of support.
- **Financial Worries:** Debt, expenses exceeding income, or unexpected bills.
- **Health Issues:** Chronic illness, injury, or concern about health conditions.
- **Major Life Changes:** Moving, changing jobs, marriage, or the loss of a loved one.

To identify your stressors, keep a stress journal. Note when you feel stressed, what caused it, and how you responded. Over time, patterns will emerge that can help you pinpoint your primary stressors.

Effective Stress Reduction Techniques

Once you have identified your stressors, you can start implementing techniques to reduce stress. Here are some effective strategies:

1. **Exercise Regularly:** Physical activity can help lower

stress levels by releasing endorphins. Aim for at least 30 minutes of moderate exercise most days.

2. **Practice Mindfulness and Meditation:** Techniques such as deep breathing, progressive muscle relaxation, and meditation can help calm the mind and reduce stress.

3. **Connect with Others:** Social support is crucial for managing stress. Spend time with friends and family, or join a support group.

4. **Prioritize and Organize:** Break tasks into smaller steps and prioritize them. Use tools like to-do lists, planners, or apps to stay organized.

5. **Set Boundaries:** Learn to say no to additional responsibilities that are not essential. Protect your time and energy.

6. **Engage in Hobbies:** Pursue activities that you enjoy and that relax you, such as reading, gardening, or playing a musical instrument.

7. **Limit Stimulants:** Reduce intake of caffeine, alcohol, and nicotine, as they can increase stress levels.

8. **Seek Professional Help:** If stress becomes overwhelming, consider talking to a therapist or counselor who can provide additional support and coping strategies.

Creating a Balanced Lifestyle

A balanced lifestyle can help prevent stress from becoming overwhelming. Here are some tips for creating balance:

- **Set Realistic Goals:** Establish achievable goals in your personal and professional life. Break larger goals into smaller, manageable steps.
- **Manage Time Effectively:** Plan your day and prioritize tasks. Delegate when possible and avoid overcommitting.
- **Practice Self-Care:** Make time for activities that nourish your mind and body, such as exercise, hobbies, and relaxation.

- **Maintain Healthy Relationships:** Cultivate supportive relationships and communicate openly with loved ones. Seek help when needed and offer support in return.
- **Develop a Positive Mindset:** Focus on what you can control and let go of what you can't. Practice gratitude and look for opportunities for personal growth in difficult situations.
- **Take Breaks:** Schedule regular breaks throughout your day to rest and recharge. Step away from work or stressful situations to clear your mind.

Creating a Stress Management Plan

A personalized stress management plan can help you proactively manage stress and maintain mental well-being. Here are some steps to create your plan:

1. **Identify Stressors:** List your primary sources of stress and how they affect you.
2. **Assess Your Current Coping Strategies:** Evaluate how you currently cope with stress. Identify what works well and what doesn't.
3. **Set Goals:** Determine what you want to achieve with your stress management plan. Be specific and realistic.
4. **Choose Stress Reduction Techniques:** Select techniques that resonate with you and fit into your lifestyle. Aim for a mix of physical, emotional, and social strategies.
5. **Create a Routine:** Incorporate stress reduction techniques into your daily routine. Consistency is key to making these practices effective.
6. **Monitor and Adjust:** Regularly assess how well your plan is working. Be open to making adjustments as needed.

By identifying your stressors and implementing effective stress reduction techniques, you can create a balanced lifestyle that supports your mental well-being. Remember, managing stress is an ongoing process, and it's important to be patient and kind to yourself as you navigate challenges.

In the next chapter, we will explore the importance of social connections and support in maintaining mental well-being.

CHAPTER 7: THE IMPORTANCE OF SOCIAL CONNECTIONS

The Role of Social Support

Social connections play a vital role in maintaining mental well-being. Positive relationships can provide emotional support, reduce stress, and enhance feelings of belonging and self-worth. Here are some ways social support benefits mental health:

- **Emotional Support:** Having people to talk to about your feelings and experiences can provide comfort and reassurance. This helps in reducing feelings of isolation and anxiety.
- **Practical Assistance:** Friends and family can offer practical help, such as assistance with tasks or advice on handling challenges.
- **Sense of Belonging:** Being part of a community or group fosters a sense of belonging and purpose, which is crucial for mental well-being.
- **Stress Relief:** Social interactions can distract you from stressors, provide opportunities for laughter, and promote relaxation.
- **Positive Influence:** Supportive relationships can encourage healthy behaviors and attitudes, such as engaging in physical activity or pursuing personal goals.

Building and Maintaining Relationships

Building and maintaining healthy relationships requires effort and intention. Here are some tips to help you cultivate strong social connections:

- **Be Open and Honest:** Share your thoughts and feelings openly with others. Authenticity fosters trust and deeper connections.
- **Listen Actively:** Pay full attention when others are speaking. Show empathy and understanding by acknowledging their feelings and experiences.
- **Show Appreciation:** Express gratitude and appreciation for the people in your life. Let them know how much they mean to you.
- **Make Time for Others:** Prioritize spending quality time with friends and family. Plan regular get-togethers, phone calls, or video chats.
- **Offer Support:** Be there for others in times of need. Offer a listening ear, practical help, or emotional support.
- **Resolve Conflicts:** Address conflicts calmly and respectfully. Focus on understanding each other's perspectives and finding mutually acceptable solutions.
- **Be Dependable:** Follow through on your commitments and be reliable. Trust is built through consistency and dependability.

Expanding Your Social Network

If you feel isolated or wish to expand your social network, consider these strategies:

- **Join Clubs or Groups:** Participate in clubs, organizations, or groups that align with your interests. This can provide opportunities to meet like-minded individuals.
- **Volunteer:** Volunteering is a great way to connect with others while contributing to your community. It can also boost your sense of purpose and self-esteem.

- **Take Classes or Workshops:** Enroll in classes or workshops to learn new skills and meet new people. This can be a great way to expand your social circle.
- **Attend Social Events:** Attend community events, social gatherings, or meetups to meet new people. Be open to new experiences and conversations.
- **Use Social Media Mindfully:** Connect with others on social media platforms, but use them mindfully. Focus on positive interactions and avoid comparisons or negative content.
- **Reconnect with Old Friends:** Reach out to old friends or acquaintances you've lost touch with. Rekindling past relationships can provide a sense of continuity and support.

Overcoming Social Anxiety

For some people, social interactions can be challenging due to social anxiety. Here are some tips to help manage social anxiety and build confidence in social settings:

- **Prepare Ahead:** Plan what you might say in social situations and practice relaxation techniques to calm your nerves.
- **Start Small:** Begin with low-pressure social situations and gradually work your way up to more challenging interactions.
- **Focus on Others:** Shift your focus from yourself to others. Ask questions and show interest in their lives to reduce self-consciousness.
- **Challenge Negative Thoughts:** Identify and challenge negative thoughts about social interactions. Replace them with positive or neutral thoughts.
- **Practice Self-Compassion:** Be kind to yourself and recognize that it's okay to feel anxious. Everyone has social anxieties at times.
- **Seek Professional Help:** If social anxiety significantly impacts your life, consider seeking help from a therapist. Cognitive-behavioral therapy (CBT) is particularly effective for social anxiety.

Nurturing Online Connections

In today's digital age, online connections can also play a significant role in social support. Here are some tips for nurturing online relationships:

- **Communicate Regularly:** Stay in touch with friends and family through regular messages, calls, or video chats.
  - **Be Mindful of Tone:** Written communication can sometimes be misinterpreted. Use emojis or clarifying statements to convey tone and intent.
- **Engage in Positive Interactions:** Share positive news, offer support, and engage in meaningful conversations.
  - **Set Boundaries:** Balance online interactions with offline activities to avoid becoming overwhelmed or disconnected from real-life relationships.
  - **Join Online Communities:** Participate in online forums, groups, or social media communities that share your interests or experiences.

By building and maintaining strong social connections, you can enhance your mental well-being and create a supportive network that helps you navigate life's challenges. Remember, quality is more important than quantity when it comes to relationships, so focus on nurturing meaningful connections.

In the next chapter, we will explore the concept of self-care and how to incorporate it into your daily routine to support your mental well-being.

CHAPTER 8: THE POWER OF SELF-CARE

Understanding Self-Care

Self-care involves taking deliberate actions to maintain and improve your physical, mental, and emotional well-being. It's about prioritizing your needs and engaging in activities that support your overall health. Self-care is not a one-time event but a continuous practice that helps you manage stress, prevent burnout, and lead a fulfilling life.

Types of Self-Care

1. **Physical Self-Care:** Activities that focus on maintaining physical health and well-being. This includes:
   - **Exercise:** Regular physical activity to improve fitness and mood.
   - **Nutrition:** Eating a balanced diet to fuel your body and mind.
   - **Sleep:** Getting adequate rest to rejuvenate your body and mind.
   - **Personal Hygiene:** Maintaining cleanliness and grooming for comfort and health.
2. **Emotional Self-Care:** Activities that support emotional well-being and resilience. This includes:
   - **Journaling:** Writing about your thoughts and feelings to process emotions and gain insight.
   - **Therapy:** Seeking professional support to work through emotional challenges.

- o **Relaxation Techniques:** Practices like deep breathing, meditation, or yoga to reduce stress.
3. **Mental Self-Care:** Activities that stimulate and challenge your mind. This includes:
    - o **Learning:** Engaging in activities that stimulate your intellect, such as reading or taking courses.
    - o **Creative Outlets:** Pursuing hobbies or creative activities that bring joy and fulfillment.
    - o **Problem-Solving:** Developing strategies to manage challenges and make decisions effectively.
4. **Social Self-Care:** Activities that nurture your relationships and social connections. This includes:
    - o **Connecting with Loved Ones:** Spending time with friends and family to strengthen bonds.
    - o **Setting Boundaries:** Establishing limits to protect your time and energy.
    - o **Seeking Support:** Asking for help when needed and offering support to others.
5. **Spiritual Self-Care:** Activities that nurture your sense of purpose and connection. This includes:
    - o **Reflection:** Spending time in contemplation or prayer to connect with your inner self.
    - o **Values Alignment:** Engaging in activities that align with your core values and beliefs.
    - o **Gratitude Practice:** Focusing on the positive aspects of your life and expressing gratitude.

Incorporating Self-Care into Your Routine

To make self-care a regular part of your life, consider the following strategies:

- **Create a Self-Care Plan:** Identify the areas of self-care that are most important to you and create a plan to incorporate them into your routine. Set specific goals and schedules for self-care activities.
- **Schedule Self-Care Time:** Treat self-care as a priority by

scheduling dedicated time for it in your calendar. This could be daily, weekly, or monthly, depending on your needs.

- **Start Small:** Begin with simple self-care activities and gradually build on them. Even small steps can make a significant difference in your well-being.
- **Be Consistent:** Consistency is key to making self-care a habit. Try to incorporate self-care activities into your daily or weekly routine to maintain balance.
- **Listen to Your Needs:** Pay attention to your physical, emotional, and mental needs and adjust your self-care practices accordingly. What works for you may change over time.
- **Practice Self-Compassion:** Be kind to yourself and recognize that self-care is not about perfection. It's about making choices that support your well-being.

Overcoming Barriers to Self-Care

Sometimes, obstacles can make it challenging to prioritize self-care. Here are some common barriers and strategies to overcome them:

- **Time Constraints:** If you feel too busy for self-care, look for small, manageable activities that can fit into your schedule. Even short breaks for relaxation or mindfulness can be effective.
- **Guilt:** Some people feel guilty about taking time for themselves. Remember that self-care is essential for maintaining your well-being and enables you to better support others.
- **Lack of Motivation:** If you're struggling to stay motivated, set achievable goals and reward yourself for making progress. Find activities that genuinely interest and inspire you.
- **Financial Constraints:** Self-care doesn't have to be expensive. Many self-care activities, such as exercise, meditation, and journaling, can be done at little to no cost.

Examples of Self-Care Activities

Here are some examples of self-care activities to inspire you:

- **Physical Self-Care:** Going for a walk, taking a relaxing bath, cooking a healthy meal, or practicing a new sport.
- **Emotional Self-Care:** Talking to a friend, writing in a journal, practicing mindfulness, or engaging in a hobby you enjoy.
- **Mental Self-Care:** Reading a book, solving puzzles, learning a new skill, or attending a workshop or seminar.
- **Social Self-Care:** Organizing a get-together with friends, joining a club, or participating in community events.
- **Spiritual Self-Care:** Attending a religious service, spending time in nature, or practicing meditation or prayer.

By incorporating self-care into your daily routine, you can enhance your overall well-being, manage stress more effectively, and lead a more balanced and fulfilling life.

In the next chapter, we will explore the importance of setting and achieving personal goals to enhance your sense of purpose and accomplishment.

CHAPTER 9: SETTING AND ACHIEVING PERSONAL GOALS

The Importance of Goal Setting

Setting and achieving personal goals is crucial for personal development and well-being. Goals provide direction, motivation, and a sense of purpose. They help you focus your efforts, measure progress, and achieve desired outcomes. Effective goal setting can:

- **Increase Motivation:** Clear goals provide motivation and a sense of accomplishment as you progress.
- **Enhance Focus:** Goals help you prioritize tasks and concentrate on what matters most.
- **Boost Confidence:** Achieving goals builds self-confidence and reinforces a sense of capability.
- **Foster Personal Growth:** Pursuing goals encourages learning, development, and self-improvement.

Types of Goals

1. **Short-Term Goals:** Goals that can be achieved within a short time frame, such as days or weeks. These often serve as stepping stones towards long-term goals. Examples include completing a project, attending a workshop, or starting a new exercise routine.
2. **Long-Term Goals:** Goals that require a longer time frame to achieve, typically spanning months or

years. These goals often involve more significant life changes or achievements. Examples include pursuing a degree, buying a house, or starting a business.

3. **Process Goals:** Goals focused on the actions and behaviors required to achieve a desired outcome. These are often within your control and can help you develop positive habits. Examples include establishing a daily routine or practicing a new skill.

4. **Outcome Goals:** Goals centered around achieving a specific result or outcome. These often measure success based on external factors. Examples include reaching a target weight, earning a promotion, or completing a marathon.

SMART Goals

To set effective goals, use the SMART criteria. SMART goals are:

- **Specific:** Clearly define what you want to achieve. The more detailed your goal, the better.
  - Example: "I want to increase my weekly exercise to 150 minutes."
- **Measurable:** Ensure your goal is quantifiable so you can track progress.
  - Example: "I will exercise for 30 minutes, five times a week."
- **Achievable:** Set realistic and attainable goals based on your current resources and constraints.
  - Example: "I will start with 10 minutes of exercise daily and gradually increase."
- **Relevant:** Align your goal with your broader objectives and values.
  - Example: "Improving my fitness will help me feel more energetic and healthier."
- **Time-Bound:** Set a deadline for achieving your goal to create urgency and focus.
  - Example: "I will achieve my target by the

end of the next three months."

Creating an Action Plan

An action plan outlines the steps needed to achieve your goals. Here's how to create one:

1. **Define Your Goal:** Start by clearly stating your goal and ensuring it meets the SMART criteria.
2. **Break Down the Goal:** Divide the goal into smaller, manageable tasks or milestones. This makes the goal less overwhelming and helps you track progress.
3. **Set Deadlines:** Establish deadlines for each task or milestone to keep yourself on track.
4. **Identify Resources:** Determine what resources or support you need to achieve your goal. This could include time, skills, tools, or assistance from others.
5. **Monitor Progress:** Regularly review your progress and adjust your action plan as needed. Celebrate small successes along the way to stay motivated.
6. **Stay Accountable:** Share your goals with a friend, mentor, or coach who can provide encouragement and hold you accountable.

Overcoming Obstacles

Challenges and setbacks are a natural part of pursuing goals. Here are strategies to overcome obstacles:

- **Anticipate Challenges:** Identify potential obstacles and plan how to address them.
- **Stay Flexible:** Be willing to adjust your plan and approach if necessary. Flexibility can help you navigate unexpected changes.
- **Maintain Persistence:** Keep a positive attitude and stay focused on your goals, even when faced with difficulties.
- **Seek Support:** Reach out to friends, family, or mentors for advice, encouragement, and support.

Evaluating and Reflecting

Once you achieve a goal, take time to evaluate your experience and reflect on what you've learned:

- **Review Your Achievements:** Assess how well you met your goal and what you accomplished.
- **Reflect on the Process:** Consider what worked well and what could be improved in your approach.
- **Celebrate Successes:** Acknowledge and celebrate your achievements to reinforce positive behavior.
- **Set New Goals:** Use your insights and experiences to set new goals and continue your personal growth journey.

By setting and achieving personal goals, you can enhance your sense of purpose, build self-confidence, and make meaningful progress in your life. Remember, goal setting is a dynamic process, and your goals may evolve over time as you grow and change.

In the next chapter, we will explore strategies for maintaining a positive mindset and cultivating resilience to navigate life's challenges effectively.

CHAPTER 10: CULTIVATING A POSITIVE MINDSET AND RESILIENCE

The Importance of a Positive Mindset

A positive mindset can significantly impact your mental well-being, overall health, and quality of life. It involves focusing on the positive aspects of life, maintaining an optimistic outlook, and approaching challenges with hope and resilience. Benefits of a positive mindset include:

- **Enhanced Problem-Solving:** A positive mindset helps you approach problems with creativity and openness, leading to better solutions.
- **Increased Resilience:** Optimism enables you to bounce back from setbacks and adapt to change more effectively.
- **Improved Health:** Positive thinking is linked to better physical health, including lower stress levels and a stronger immune system.
- **Greater Happiness:** Focusing on positive experiences and achievements can enhance your overall sense of well-being and life satisfaction.

Strategies for Developing a Positive Mindset

1. **Practice Gratitude:** Regularly acknowledging and appreciating the positive aspects of your life can shift your focus from what's lacking to what's abundant. Keep a gratitude journal where you write down things you're thankful for each day.

2. **Reframe Negative Thoughts:** Challenge and reframe negative thoughts to see situations from a more positive perspective. For example, instead of thinking, "I failed," try, "I learned something valuable from this experience."

3. **Surround Yourself with Positivity:** Engage with people who uplift and inspire you. Avoid negative influences and seek out supportive relationships that encourage a positive outlook.

4. **Engage in Positive Self-Talk:** Replace self-criticism with encouraging and affirming statements. Be kind and supportive to yourself, just as you would to a friend.

5. **Set Realistic Goals:** Establish achievable goals that give you a sense of purpose and accomplishment. Celebrate your successes, no matter how small.

6. **Focus on Solutions:** When faced with challenges, concentrate on finding solutions rather than dwelling on problems. Take proactive steps to address issues and move forward.

7. **Practice Mindfulness:** Mindfulness techniques, such as meditation and deep breathing, can help you stay present and reduce negative thinking.

8. **Engage in Activities You Enjoy:** Pursue hobbies and activities that bring you joy and fulfillment. Engaging in enjoyable activities can boost your mood and overall outlook.

Building Resilience

Resilience is the ability to adapt to adversity, recover from setbacks, and continue moving forward. Developing resilience involves cultivating specific skills and attitudes. Here's how you can build resilience:

1. **Develop a Growth Mindset:** Embrace challenges as opportunities for growth and learning. Believe that you can develop your abilities through effort and perseverance.
2. **Build Strong Relationships:** Cultivate a network of supportive friends, family, and colleagues who can provide emotional support and encouragement during difficult times.
3. **Practice Self-Care:** Prioritize self-care activities that maintain your physical, emotional, and mental well-being. Taking care of yourself strengthens your ability to cope with stress.
4. **Maintain Flexibility:** Be adaptable and open to change. Flexibility helps you adjust to new circumstances and find alternative solutions when faced with obstacles.
5. **Set Realistic Expectations:** Set achievable goals and manage your expectations. Understand that setbacks are a normal part of life and use them as learning experiences.
6. **Focus on What You Can Control:** Concentrate on aspects of your life that are within your control and let go of what you cannot change. This helps reduce feelings of helplessness.
7. **Seek Support:** Don't hesitate to seek help from professionals, such as therapists or counselors, if needed. Professional support can provide valuable tools and strategies for building resilience.
8. **Cultivate Optimism:** Focus on positive outcomes and maintain hope for the future. Optimism helps you persevere through difficulties and stay motivated.

Practical Exercises for Cultivating Positivity and Resilience

1. **Gratitude Practice:** Spend a few minutes each

day listing three things you're grateful for. Reflect on why you appreciate these things and how they contribute to your well-being.

2. **Reframing Exercise:** When faced with a negative thought, write it down and then reframe it into a more positive or constructive thought. For example, "I'm not good at this" can be reframed as "I'm learning and improving with practice."

3. **Resilience Journal:** Keep a journal where you record challenges you've faced, how you handled them, and what you learned from the experience. Review it periodically to see how you've grown.

4. **Mindfulness Meditation:** Practice mindfulness meditation for a few minutes each day to center yourself and reduce stress. Focus on your breath and observe your thoughts without judgment.

5. **Positive Affirmations:** Write down positive affirmations that resonate with you and repeat them daily. Affirmations can help reinforce a positive mindset and boost self-confidence.

By cultivating a positive mindset and building resilience, you can navigate life's challenges with greater ease and maintain a sense of well-being and hope. Remember, developing these qualities is an ongoing process, and consistency is key.

In the next chapter, we will explore the impact of lifestyle choices on mental well-being and how to make choices that support a balanced and fulfilling life.

THE IMPACT OF LIFESTYLE CHOICES ON MENTAL WELL-BEING

Understanding the Connection Between Lifestyle and Mental Well-Being

Your lifestyle choices significantly impact your mental well-being. Daily habits and routines influence your physical health, emotional state, and overall quality of life. Making intentional choices that support a healthy lifestyle can enhance your mental well-being and contribute to a more balanced, fulfilling life.

Key Lifestyle Choices and Their Impact

1. **Diet and Nutrition**
   - **Balanced Diet:** Eating a variety of nutrient-rich foods supports brain function and mood regulation. Incorporate fruits, vegetables, whole grains, lean proteins, and healthy fats into your diet.
   - **Hydration:** Staying hydrated is essential for cognitive function and emotional stability. Aim to drink plenty of water throughout the day.
   - **Limit Processed Foods:** Reduce consumption of processed foods high in sugar, salt, and unhealthy fats, as they can negatively affect mood and energy levels.
2. **Physical Activity**
   - **Regular Exercise:** Engaging in regular physical activity releases endorphins, which improve mood and reduce stress. Aim for at least 150 minutes of moderate exercise or 75 minutes of vigorous exercise per week.
   - **Movement Breaks:** Incorporate short bursts of physical activity throughout your day, especially if you have a sedentary job. This helps reduce stress and improve focus.
3. **Sleep Quality**
   - **Consistent Sleep Schedule:** Establish a regular sleep routine by going to bed and waking up at the same time each day. This helps regulate your

body's internal clock and improves sleep quality.

- o **Sleep Environment:** Create a restful sleep environment by keeping your bedroom cool, dark, and quiet. Avoid screens and stimulating activities before bedtime.

4. **Work-Life Balance**

- o **Set Boundaries:** Establish clear boundaries between work and personal life to prevent burnout. Designate specific times for work and leisure and avoid working beyond those hours.
- o **Prioritize Downtime:** Make time for relaxation and activities that bring you joy. Balance your workload with hobbies, social interactions, and self-care.

5. **Social Connections**

- o **Maintain Relationships:** Foster and nurture relationships with family, friends, and colleagues. Positive social interactions contribute to emotional support and overall well-being.
- o **Engage in Community:** Participate in community events or groups that align with your interests. Building a sense of belonging enhances mental health.

6. **Stress Management**

- o **Develop Coping Strategies:** Implement stress reduction techniques such as mindfulness, meditation, or deep breathing exercises. Regular practice helps manage stress and improves mental clarity.
- o **Seek Help When Needed:** Don't hesitate to seek professional support if stress becomes overwhelming. Therapy or counseling can provide valuable tools for managing stress effectively.

7. **Healthy Habits**

- o **Limit Substance Use:** Reduce or avoid the use of alcohol, tobacco, and recreational drugs, as they can negatively impact mental and physical health.
- o **Practice Mindfulness:** Incorporate mindfulness practices into your daily routine

to stay present and manage stress.

Creating a Healthy Lifestyle Plan

To create a lifestyle plan that supports your
mental well-being, follow these steps:

1. **Assess Your Current Lifestyle:** Evaluate your current habits and routines to identify areas that may impact your mental well-being. Consider aspects such as diet, exercise, sleep, and work-life balance.
2. **Set Realistic Goals:** Establish achievable goals for making positive lifestyle changes. Start with small, manageable changes and gradually build on them.
3. **Develop an Action Plan:** Create a plan that outlines specific actions you will take to improve your lifestyle. Include steps for incorporating healthy habits into your daily routine.
4. **Monitor Progress:** Track your progress and make adjustments as needed. Use tools such as journals or apps to record your habits and reflect on your achievements.
5. **Stay Motivated:** Find ways to stay motivated and accountable, such as setting reminders, seeking support from friends or family, or rewarding yourself for reaching milestones.

Maintaining Lifestyle Changes

Maintaining lifestyle changes requires consistency and commitment. Here are some tips to help you stay on track:

- **Build Habits Gradually:** Focus on one or two changes at a time to avoid becoming overwhelmed. Gradually integrate new habits into your routine.
- **Be Patient:** Understand that lasting changes take time. Be patient with yourself and celebrate small victories along the way.
- **Adapt as Needed:** Life circumstances and priorities may

change, so be flexible and adapt your plan as needed. Adjust your goals and strategies to fit your evolving needs.

- **Seek Support:** Connect with others who share similar goals or interests. Supportive relationships can provide encouragement and accountability.

By making intentional lifestyle choices that support your mental well-being, you can create a foundation for a healthier, more balanced life. Remember that small, consistent changes can lead to significant improvements over time.

Recap of Key Points

Chapter 1: Introduction to Mental Well-Being

- Mental well-being is integral to overall health.
- It encompasses emotional, psychological, and social aspects.
- Understanding and addressing mental well-being can improve life quality and functionality.

Chapter 2: Understanding Emotional Health

- Emotional health involves self-awareness and emotional intelligence.
- Managing emotions effectively is crucial for maintaining emotional balance.
- Techniques include self-reflection, emotional regulation, and seeking support when needed.

Chapter 3: Building Resilience

- Resilience helps individuals adapt to adversity and bounce back from setbacks.
- Key strategies include developing a growth mindset, building strong relationships, and maintaining flexibility.
- Resilience can be cultivated through positive self-talk and problem-solving skills.

Chapter 4: Effective Stress Management

- Stress management techniques include mindfulness, exercise, and time management.
- Identifying stressors and developing coping strategies are essential for managing stress.
- Regular practice of relaxation techniques can reduce stress and improve well-being.

Chapter 5: The Role of Relationships

- Positive relationships contribute

significantly to mental well-being.
- Healthy relationships provide support, enhance emotional stability, and foster personal growth.
- Effective communication and setting boundaries are crucial for maintaining healthy relationships.

Chapter 6: Mindfulness and Meditation

- Mindfulness and meditation practices help manage stress and improve mental clarity.
- Regular practice can lead to increased self-awareness and emotional regulation.
- Techniques include deep breathing, body scans, and mindful observation.

Chapter 7: The Importance of Healthy Boundaries

- Healthy boundaries protect personal space and emotional health.
- Setting and maintaining boundaries involves clear communication and self-respect.
- Boundaries help prevent burnout and maintain balanced relationships.

Chapter 8: The Power of Self-Care

- Self-care involves activities that support physical, emotional, and mental health.
- Key areas include physical exercise, emotional reflection, and social connections.
- Incorporating self-care into daily life is crucial for long-term well-being.

Chapter 9: Setting and Achieving Personal Goals

- Effective goal setting involves defining specific, measurable, achievable, relevant, and time-bound (SMART) goals.
- Creating an action plan and monitoring progress are essential for goal achievement.
- Reflecting on goals and adjusting plans as needed

helps maintain direction and motivation.

Chapter 10: Cultivating a Positive Mindset and Resilience

- A positive mindset enhances motivation, focus, and overall happiness.
- Building resilience involves developing a growth mindset, seeking support, and practicing optimism.
- Strategies include gratitude practices, reframing negative thoughts, and maintaining flexibility in the face of challenges.

This recap highlights the essential elements from each chapter, focusing on practical strategies for improving and maintaining mental well-being.

Encouragement for Ongoing Self-Care

Taking care of yourself is not a one-time effort but an ongoing journey. Self-care is essential for maintaining your mental, emotional, and physical well-being. Here's a reminder to keep prioritizing self-care as a regular part of your life:

1. Embrace the Journey: Self-care is a continuous process of understanding and meeting your own needs. Celebrate the small victories and recognize that every step you take towards self-care contributes to your overall well-being.

2. Prioritize Yourself: You are worthy of care and attention. Make self-care a non-negotiable part of your routine, just as you would with other important commitments. Remember, taking care of yourself allows you to be at your best for others as well.

3. Listen to Your Needs: Tune into your body and mind. Pay attention to signals of stress, fatigue, or imbalance and respond with compassion. Adjust your self-care practices as needed to address your evolving needs.

4. Be Consistent: Consistency is key to effective self-care. Incorporate self-care practices into your daily or weekly routine to build lasting habits. Even small, regular actions can have a significant impact over time.

5. Seek Balance: Strive for a balance between different aspects of self-care, including physical health, emotional well-being, social connections, and relaxation. A well-rounded approach helps maintain overall harmony and prevents burnout.

6. Practice Self-Compassion: Be kind to yourself, especially during challenging times. Self-care is not about perfection but about taking thoughtful, loving actions to support your well-being. Forgive yourself for any lapses and recommit to your self-care journey.

7. Make It Enjoyable: Choose self-care activities that bring you joy and satisfaction. Whether it's a hobby, a relaxing bath, or spending time with loved ones, make sure your self-care practices are enjoyable and fulfilling.

8. Set Boundaries: Protect your self-care time by setting healthy boundaries with work, social obligations, and other responsibilities. Create space for yourself and honor it as an essential aspect of your well-being.

9. Reflect and Adjust: Periodically reflect on your self-care practices and their impact on your well-being. Adjust your approach as needed to ensure it aligns with your current needs and goals.

10. Celebrate Your Efforts: Acknowledge and celebrate your commitment to self-care. Recognizing the positive changes and improvements in your life reinforces the importance of ongoing self-care and motivates you to continue.

Remember, self-care is a lifelong commitment and a vital part of living a balanced and fulfilling life. By consistently prioritizing your well-being, you are investing in your health, happiness, and overall quality of life. Keep nurturing yourself, and you will continue to thrive and grow.

Resources for Further Reading and Support

Books:

1. **"The Self-Care Solution: A Modern Guide to Whole Body Wellness"** by Jennifer Ashton, MD
   - A comprehensive guide to self-care practices and strategies for improving overall well-being.
2. **"Atomic Habits: An Easy & Proven Way to Build Good Habits & Break Bad Ones"** by James Clear
   - Offers practical advice on habit formation and maintaining positive lifestyle changes.
3. **"Mindfulness for Beginners: Reclaiming the Present Moment—and Your Life"** by Jon Kabat-Zinn
   - An introduction to mindfulness and meditation techniques for reducing stress and enhancing mental well-being.
4. **"Resilient: How to Grow an Unshakable Core of Calm, Strength, and Happiness"** by Rick Hanson, PhD
   - Explores strategies for building resilience and developing a positive mindset.
5. **"The Gifts of Imperfection: Let Go of Who You Think You're Supposed to Be and Embrace Who You Are"** by Brené Brown
   - Encourages self-compassion and embracing vulnerability as pathways to emotional health and fulfillment.

Websites and Online Resources:

1. **National Institute of Mental Health (NIMH)**
   - www.nimh.nih.gov
   - Provides information on mental health conditions, treatments, and research.
2. **Mindful**

o www.mindful.org

o Offers resources, articles, and practices related to mindfulness and meditation.

3. **American Psychological Association (APA)**

o www.apa.org

o Features articles, research, and resources on psychological health and well-being.

4. **Headspace**

o www.headspace.com

o Provides guided meditations and mindfulness practices for stress management and mental clarity.

5. **Therapy Directory**

o www.therapy-directory.org.uk

o A resource for finding qualified therapists and counselors for various mental health concerns.

Podcasts:

1. **"The Happiness Lab with Dr. Laurie Santos"**

o Explores the science of happiness and practical tips for improving well-being.

2. **"Therapy Chat"**

o Focuses on mental health topics, therapy practices, and personal growth.

3. **"On Being with Krista Tippett"**

o Discusses deep questions about meaning, faith, and the human experience.

Support Organizations:

1. **Mental Health America (MHA)**

o www.mhanational.org

o Provides resources, tools, and support for mental health and well-being.

2. **National Alliance on Mental Illness (NAMI)**

o www.nami.org

o Offers support, education, and advocacy for individuals and families affected by mental illness.

3. **The Substance Abuse and Mental Health Services Administration (SAMHSA)**
   - www.samhsa.gov
   - Provides resources and support for mental health and substance use disorders.
   - These resources offer valuable information, practical advice, and support to further your understanding of mental well-being and enhance your self-care practices.

www.ingramcontent.com/pod-product-compliance
Lightning Source LLC
Chambersburg PA
CBHW051704250726

48653CB00007B/2834